MOVIE SONGS FOR UKULELE

2 **City of Stars** La La Land

5 **Cups (When I'm Gone)** Pitch Perfect

13 **Evermore** Beauty and the Beast

8 **Falling Slowly** Once

10 **Ghostbusters** Ghostbusters

25 **Hallelujah** Shrek

18 **Happy** Despicable Me 2

22 **I Will Always Love You** The Bodyguard

28 **It Might Be You** Tootsie

31 **Mrs. Robinson** The Graduate

34 **Theme from "New York, New York"** New York, New York

36 **Oh, Pretty Woman** Pretty Woman

40 **Old Time Rock & Roll** Risky Business

46 **Over the Rainbow** The Wizard of Oz

43 **The Rainbow Connection** The Muppet Movie

63 **Shout** Animal House

48 **Somewhere Out There** An American Tail

50 **That's Amore (That's Love)** The Caddy

52 **That's What Friends Are For** Night Shift

54 **Time Warp** The Rocky Horror Picture Show

60 **Twist and Shout** Ferris Bueller's Day Off

70 **What the World Needs Now Is Love** My Best Friend's Wedding

78 **The Wind Beneath My Wings** Beaches

72 **The Windmills of Your Mind** The Thomas Crown Affair

76 **You Light Up My Life** You Light Up My Life

ISBN 978-1-5400-2338-4

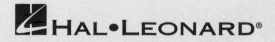

Visit Hal Leonard Online at
www.halleonard.com

Contact Us:
Hal Leonard
7777 West Bluemound Road
Milwaukee, WI 53213
Email: info@halleonard.com

In Europe contact:
Hal Leonard Europe Limited
Distribution Centre, Newmarket Road
Bury St Edmunds, Suffolk, IP33 3YB
Email: info@halleonardeurope.com

In Australia contact:
Hal Leonard Australia Pty. Ltd.
4 Lentara Court
Cheltenham, Victoria, 3192 Australia
Email: info@halleonard.com.au

City of Stars

from LA LA LAND
Music by Justin Hurwitz
Lyrics by Benj Pasek & Justin Paul

wants, there in the bars ___

and through the smoke-screen of the crowd - ed res - tau - rants: ___ it's

love. Yes, all we're look-ing for is love from some - one else. _

___ *Sebastian:* A rush, *Mia:* a glance, *Sebastian:* a touch, *Mia:* a dance. *Both:* A

Bridge

look in some-bod-y's eyes ___ to light up the skies, ___ to o - pen the world _

___ and send it reel-ing. A voice that says, "I'll be here, ___ and you'll be al - right." _

Cups
(When I'm Gone)

from the Motion Picture Soundtrack PITCH PERFECT
Words and Music by A.P. Carter, Luisa Gerstein and Heloise Tunstall-Behrens

miss me by my hair, ___ you'll miss me ev - 'ry - where. ___ Oh,
miss me by my walk, ___ you're gon - na miss me by my talk. ___ Oh,

you're gon - na miss ___ me when I'm gone. When I'm
you're gon - na miss ___ me when I'm gone. When I'm

gone, when I'm gone, _____ you're gon - na miss ___ me when I'm
gone, when I'm gone, _____ you're gon - na miss ___ me when I'm

gone. You're gon - na miss me by my walk, ___ you're gon - na
gone. You're gon - na miss me by my hair, ___ you're gon - na

To Coda

miss me by my talk. ___ Oh, ___ you're gon - na miss ___ me when I'm
miss me ev - 'ry - where. ___ Oh, ___ you're sure gon - na miss me when I'm

Verse

gone. 2. I got my tick - et for the long way ___ 'round,

the one with the pret-ti-est ___ of views. It's got

moun-tains, it's got riv-ers, it's got sights to give you shiv-ers, ___ but it

D.S. al Coda

Coda

sure would be pret-ti-er ___ with you. When I'm

gone. When I'm

Outro-Chorus

gone, when I'm gone, ___ you're gon-na miss ___ me when I'm

gone. You're gon-na miss me by my walk, ___ you're gon-na

miss me by my talk. ___ Oh, you're gon-na miss ___ me when I'm gone.

Falling Slowly

from the Motion Picture ONCE
Words and Music by Glen Hansard and Marketa Irglova

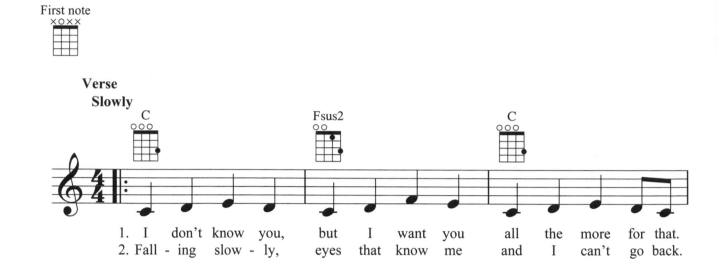

1. I don't know you, but I want you all the more for that.
2. Fall - ing slow - ly, eyes that know me and I can't go back.

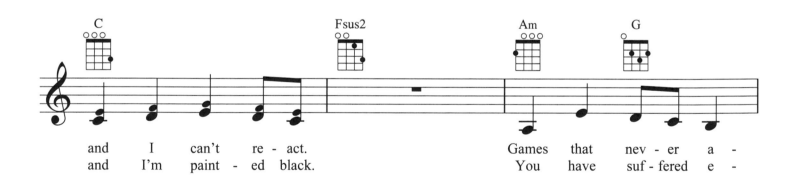

Words fall through me and al - ways fool me,
Moods that take me and e - rase me,

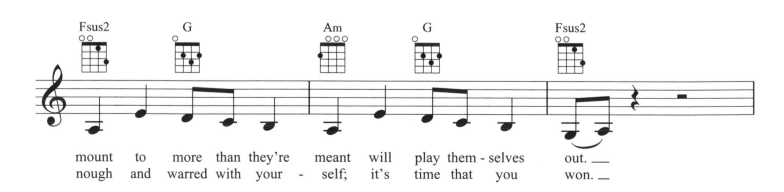

and I can't re - act.
and I'm paint - ed black.

Games that nev - er a -
You have suf - fered e -

mount to more than they're meant will play them - selves out. __
nough and warred with your - self; it's time that you won. __

Ghostbusters

from the Columbia Motion Picture GHOSTBUSTERS
Words and Music by Ray Parker, Jr.

(Spoken:) I ain't 'fraid of no ghost!

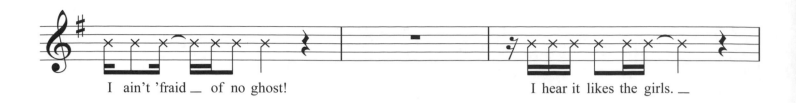

I ain't 'fraid __ of no ghost!   I hear it likes the girls. __

I ain't 'fraid __ of no ghost!   Yeah, yeah, yeah, yeah.

2.

G   F   C   **Interlude**
N.C.

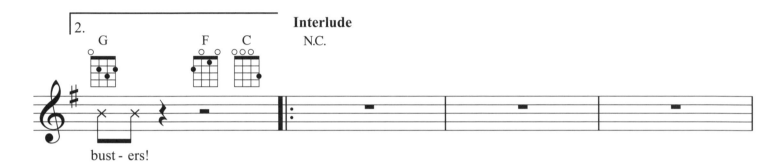

bust - ers!

1.   **2.**   *D.S. al Coda*
(take 2nd ending)

Bust - in' makes me feel good! _____

⊕ **Coda**   **Outro**   *Repeat ad lib. and fade*

G   F   C   G   F   C   G   F   C

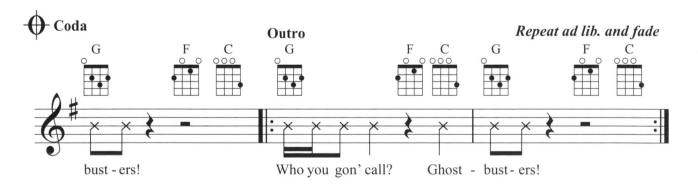

bust - ers!   Who you gon' call?   Ghost - bust - ers!

Additional Lyrics

4. Who you gon' call? *(Ghostbusters!)*
   Mm, if you have a dose of a freaky ghost, baby, you'd better call *(Ghostbusters!)*

(D.S.) Don't get caught alone, oh no. *(Ghostbusters!)*
   When it comes through your door,
   Unless you just want some more, I think you better call *(Ghostbusters!)*

Evermore

from BEAUTY AND THE BEAST
Music by Alan Menken
Lyrics by Tim Rice

tow - er, _____ wait - ing by ____ an o - pen

door, I'll fool my - self she'll walk right

in, and be with me _____ for ev - er -

more.

Verse

2. I rage a - gainst ___ the trials of love.

I curse the fad - ing _____ of the light.

Though she's al - read - y flown __ so far be - yond my reach,

she's nev - er out of sight. _____

Chorus

Now I know she'll nev - er

leave me, e - ven as she fades from view. She will

still in - spire __ me, be a part __ of ev - 'ry - thing __ I

do. Wast - ing in my lone - ly tow - er,

Happy

from DESPICABLE ME 2
Words and Music by Pharrell Williams

_____ you feel ____ like that's what you wan - na do. _____

𝄋 Bridge

N.C.(A7)

Bring me down, _____ can't noth - in' bring me down; _

_____ your love is too high. Bring me down, _____ can't noth - in'

1.

bring me down. _____ (Let me tell you now.)

Chorus

2., 3.

Fmaj7

_____ I said... (Be - cause I'm hap - py.) Clap a - long if _____

Em7   A7

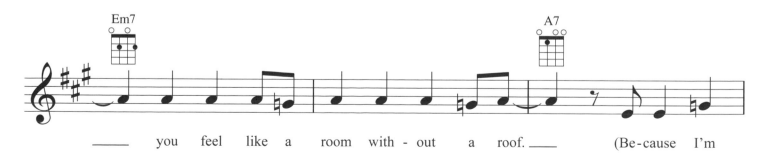

_____ you feel like a room with - out a roof. _____ (Be - cause I'm

I Will Always Love You

featured in THE BODYGUARD
Words and Music by Dolly Parton

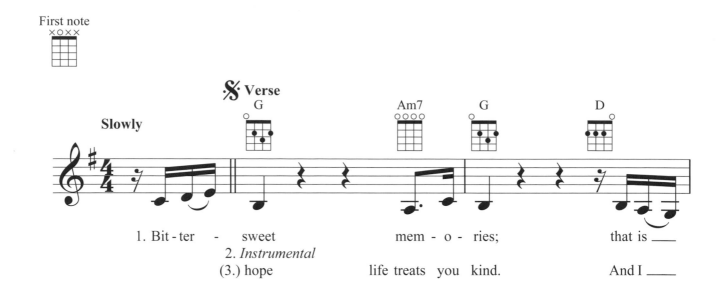

1. Bit - ter - sweet mem - o - ries; that is ___
2. *Instrumental*
(3.) hope life treats you kind. And I ___

all ___ I'm tak - ing ___ with me. ___ So, good -

hope ___ you have all ___ you've dreamed ___ of. ___ And I

byc. ___ Please, don't ___ cry. We both ___

wish to you joy and hap - pi - ness. But a - bove

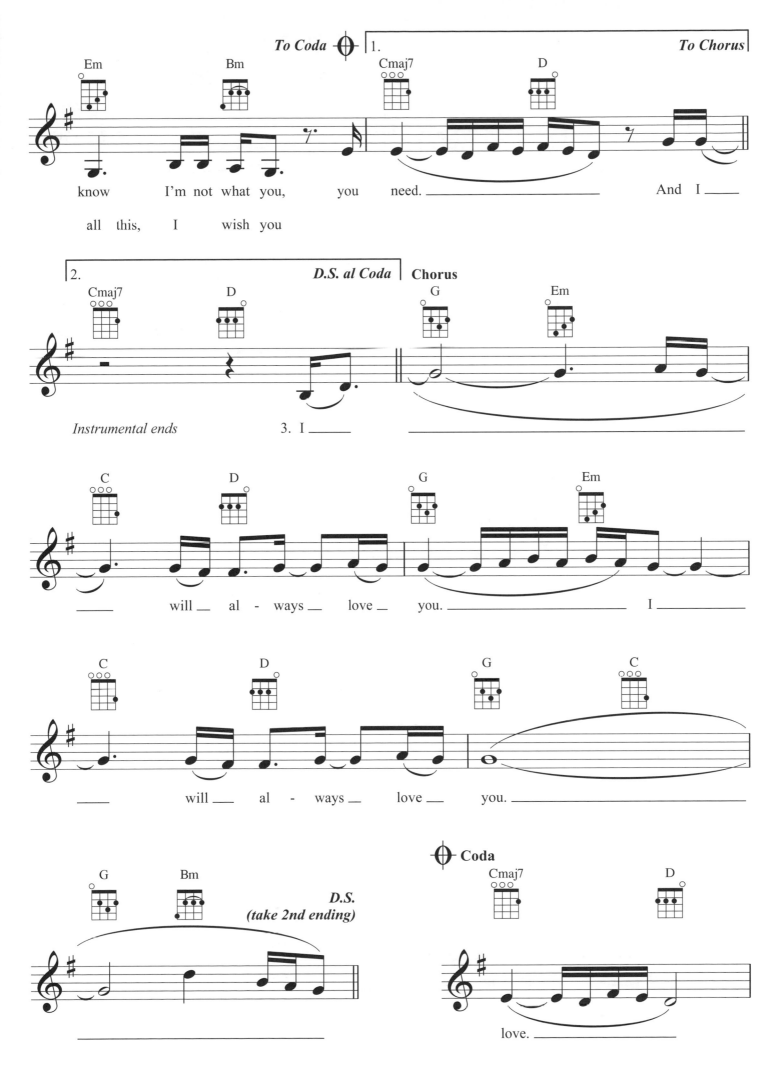

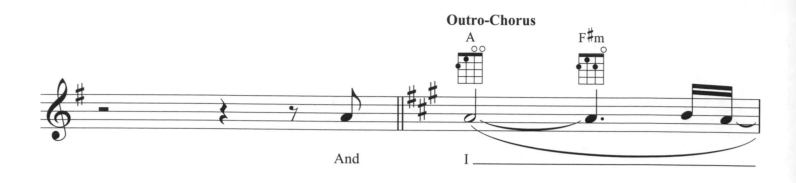

And   I _____

_____ will _ al - ways _ love _ you. _____ I _____ will al -

- ways _____ love _ you.   I _____ will al -

- ways _____ love _ you. _____ I _____ will al -

- ways _____ love _ you.

Hallelujah

featured in the DreamWorks Motion Picture SHREK
Words and Music by Leonard Cohen

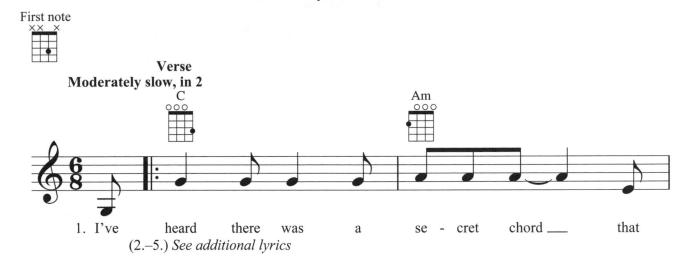

1. I've heard there was a se - cret chord ____ that
(2.–5.) *See additional lyrics*

Da - vid played _ and it pleased the Lord, __ but you don't ____ real - ly

care for mu - sic, ____ do ya? ____ It

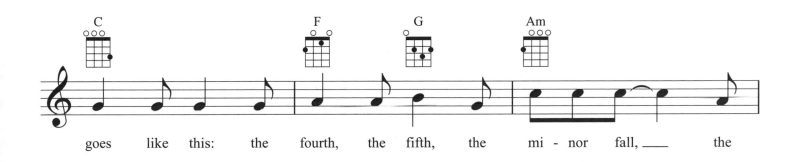

goes like this: the fourth, the fifth, the mi - nor fall, ____ the

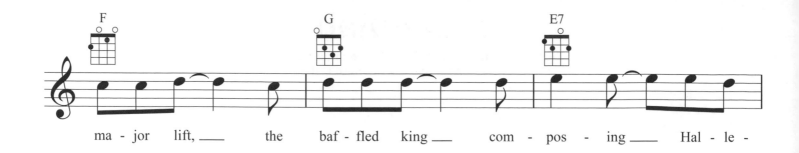

ma - jor lift, ____ the baf - fled king ____ com - pos - ing ____ Hal - le -

Chorus

lu - jah. _____ Hal - le - lu - jah, _____ hal - le -

lu - jah, _____ hal - le - lu - jah, _____ hal - le -

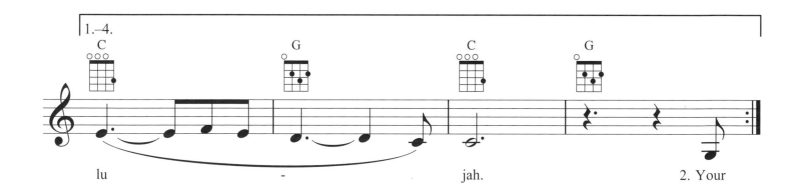

lu - jah. 2. Your

Outro-Chorus

lu - jah. Hal - le - lu - jah. _____ Hal - le -

lu - jah. _____ Hal - le - lu - jah. _____ Hal - le -

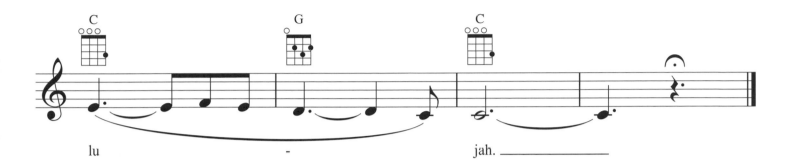

lu - jah. _____

Additional Lyrics

2. Your faith was strong but you needed proof.
   You saw her bathing on the roof.
   Her beauty and the moonlight overthrew ya.
   She tied you to a kitchen chair.
   She broke your throne, she cut your hair.
   And from your lips she drew the Hallelujah.

3. Maybe I have been here before.
   I know this room, I've walked this floor.
   I used to live alone before I knew ya.
   I've seen your flag on the marble arch.
   Love is not a vict'ry march.
   It's a cold and it's a broken Hallelujah.

4. There was a time you let me know
   What's real and going on below.
   But now you never show it to me, do ya?
   And remember when I moved in you.
   The holy dark was movin', too,
   And every breath we drew was Hallelujah.

5. Maybe there's a God above,
   And all I ever learned from love
   Was how to shoot at someone who outdrew ya.
   And it's not a cry you can hear at night.
   It's not somebody who's seen the light.
   It's a cold and it's a broken Hallelujah.

It Might Be You

Theme from TOOTSIE
Words by Alan and Marilyn Bergman
Music by Dave Grusin

Chorus

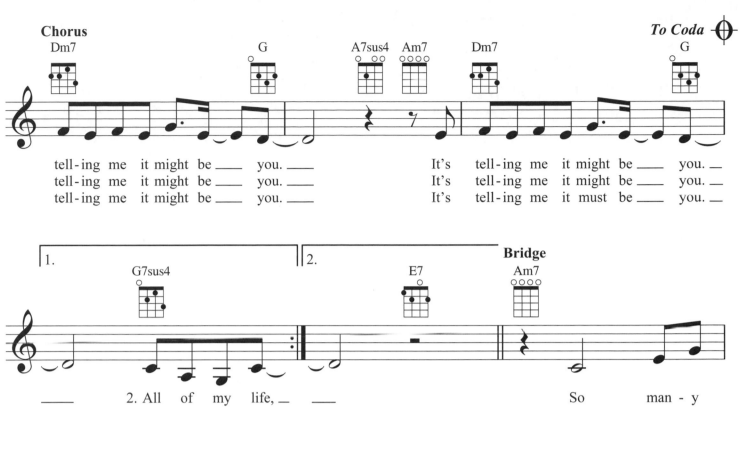

tell-ing me it might be ___ you. ___
tell-ing me it might be ___ you. ___
tell-ing me it might be ___ you. ___

It's tell-ing me it might be ___ you. __
It's tell-ing me it might be ___ you. __
It's tell-ing me it must be ___ you. __

1. **2.** **Bridge**

___ 2. All of my life, _ ___

So man-y

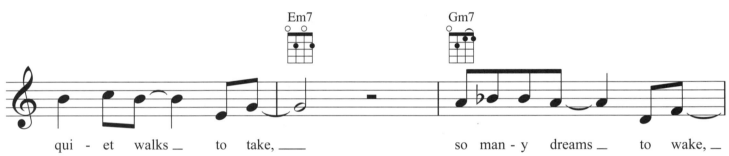

qui-et walks _ to take, ___ so man-y dreams _ to wake, _

___ and we've so much love _ to make. _

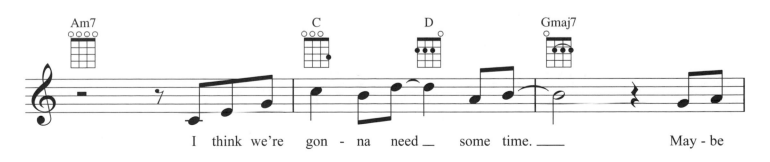

I think we're gon-na need _ some time. ___ May-be

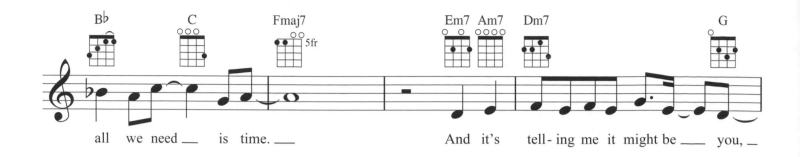

all we need ___ is time. ___   And it's   tell-ing me it might be ___ you, ___

___   all of my life. ___

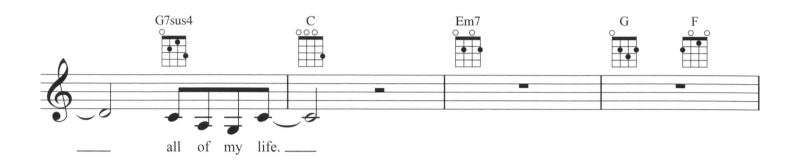

D.S. al Coda

3. I've been   ___   And I'm

Coda

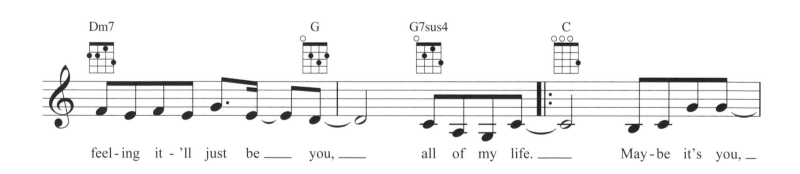

feel-ing it-'ll just be ___ you, ___   all of my life. ___   May-be it's you, ___

Repeat and fade

___   may-be it's you ___   I've been wait - ing for all of my life. ___

Mrs. Robinson

from THE GRADUATE
Words and Music by Paul Simon

First note

Moderately bright, in 2

𝄋 **Chorus**

And here's to you, _____ Mrs. _ Rob - in - son. _____

(D.S.) *See additional lyrics*

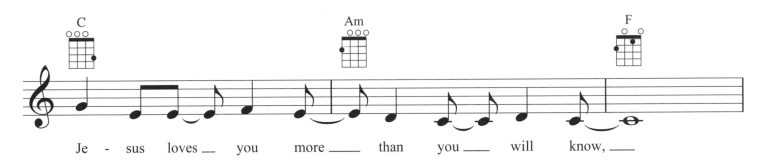

Je - sus loves _ you more _____ than you _ will know, _____

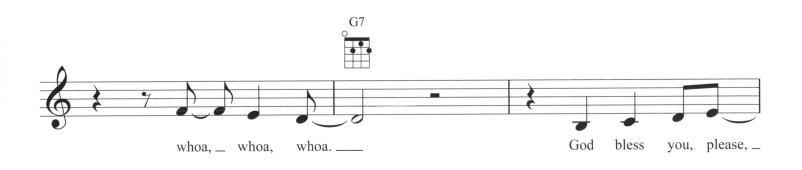

whoa, _ whoa, whoa. _____ God bless you, please, _

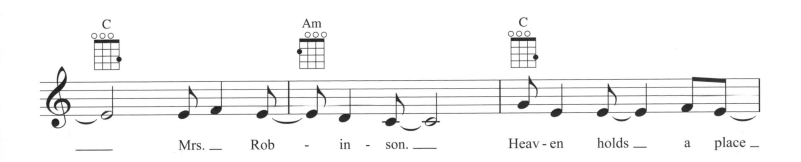

_____ Mrs. _ Rob - in - son. _____ Heav - en holds _ a place _

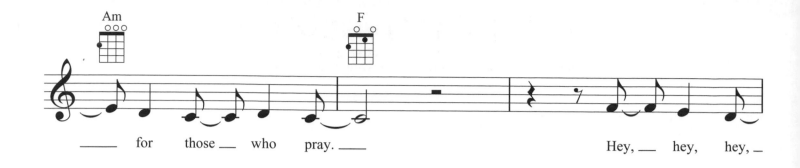

_____ for those _____ who pray. _____ Hey, _____ hey, hey, _____

To Coda ✛

_____ hey, _____ hey, hey. _____

Verse

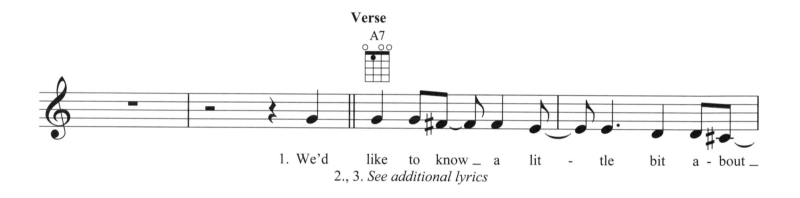

1. We'd like to know _____ a lit - tle bit a - bout _____
2., 3. *See additional lyrics*

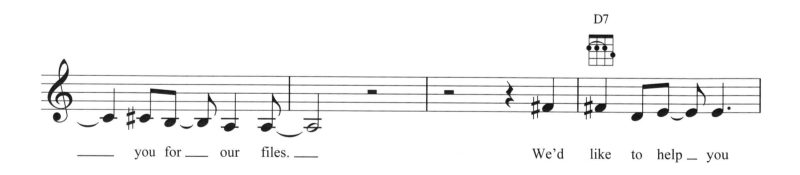

_____ you for _____ our files. _____ We'd like to help _____ you

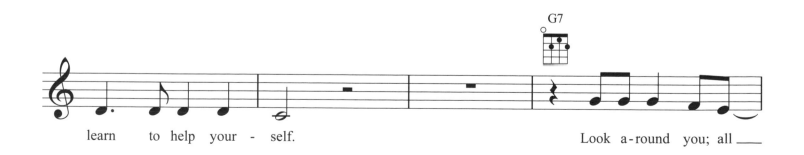

learn to help your - self. Look a - round you; all _____

_____ you see _____ are sym - pa - thet - ic eyes. _____

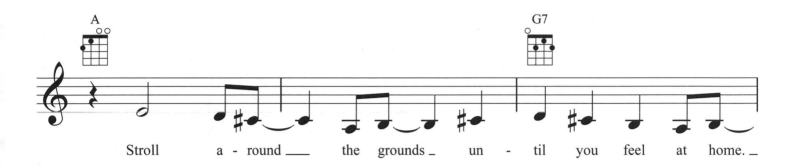

Stroll a - round _____ the grounds _ un - til you feel at home. _

Coda

| 1., 2. | | 3. | **D.S. al Coda** |

_____ { And here's to you, _ Koo, koo, ka - choo, _ } Where have you gone, _ _____

Additional Lyrics

2. Hide it in a hiding place where no one ever goes.
   Put it in your pantry with your cupcakes.
   It's a little secret, just the Robinsons' affair.
   Most of all, you've got to hide it from the kids.

3. Sitting on a sofa on a Sunday afternoon,
   Going to the candidates' debate.
   Laugh about it, shout about it when you've got to choose.
   Ev'ry way you look at this, you lose.

Last Chorus: Where have you gone, Joe DiMaggio?
   A nation turns its lonely eyes to you, woo, woo, woo.
   What's that you say, Mrs. Robinson?
   Joltin' Joe has left and gone away,
   Hey, hey, hey, hey, hey, hey.

Theme from "New York, New York"

from NEW YORK, NEW YORK
Words by Fred Ebb
Music by John Kander

First note

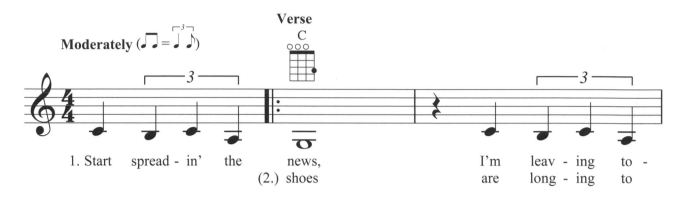

1. Start spread-in' the news,   I'm leav-ing to-
(2.) shoes   are long-ing to

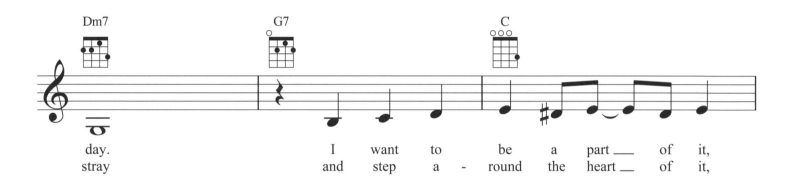

day.   I want to be a part ___ of it,
stray   and step a-round the heart ___ of it,

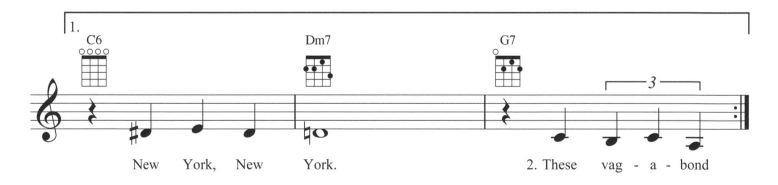

New York, New York.   2. These vag-a-bond

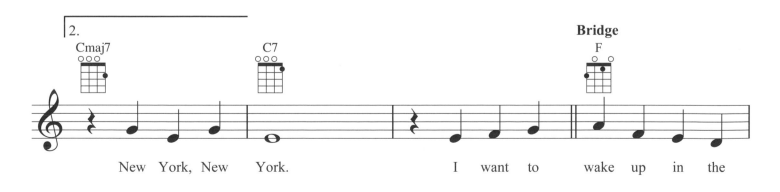

New York, New York.   I want to wake up in the

cit - y that does - n't sleep to find I'm

king of the hill, _____ top of the heap. 3. My lit - tle town

Verse

blues are melt - ing a - way. I'll make a

brand - new start __ of it, in old New York. If I can

Outro

make it there, __ I'd make it an - y - where. __ It's up to

you, New York, New York. _____

Oh, Pretty Woman

featured in the Motion Picture PRETTY WOMAN
Words and Music by Roy Orbison and Bill Dees

First note

Verse
Moderate Rock

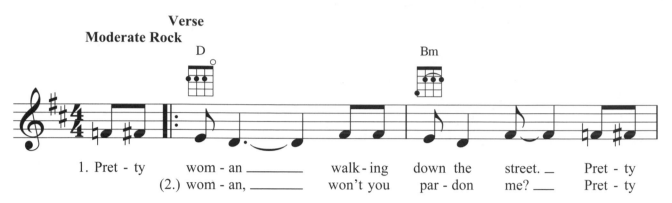

1. Pret - ty wom - an _____ walk - ing down the street. _ Pret - ty
(2.) wom - an, _____ won't you par - don me? _ Pret - ty

wom - an, the kind I like to meet. _ Pret - ty
wom - an, I could - n't help but see, _ pret - ty

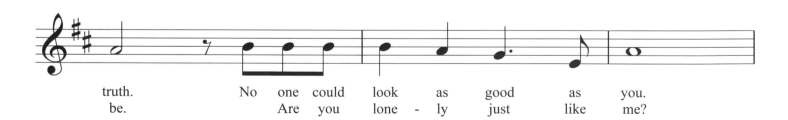

wom - an, _____ I don't be - lieve you; _____ you're not the
wom - an, _____ that you look love - ly _____ as can

truth. No one could look as good as you.
be. Are you lone - ly just like me?

Bridge

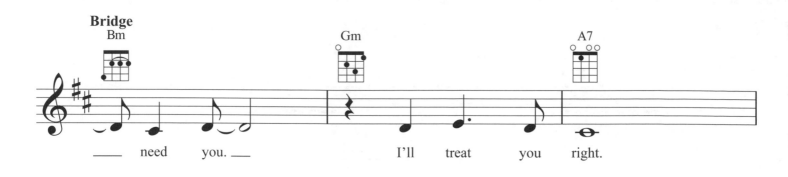

_____ need you. _____ I'll treat you right.

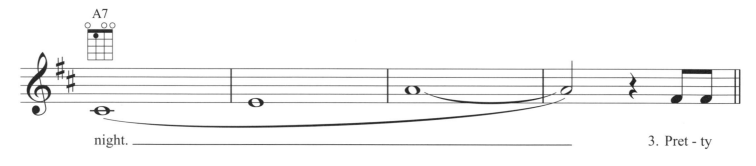

Come with me, ba - by; _____ be mine to -

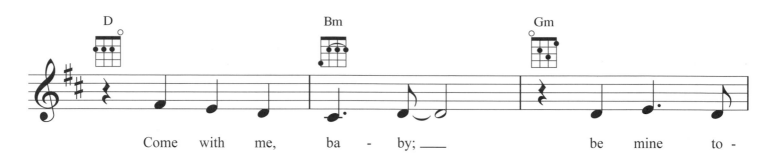

night. _____ 3. Pret - ty

Verse

wom - an, _____ don't walk on by. _____ Pret - ty wom - an, _____ don't

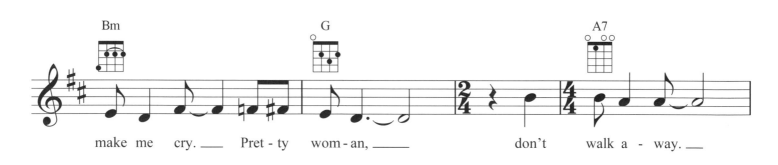

make me cry. _____ Pret - ty wom - an, _____ don't walk a - way. _____

Hey, o - kay. If that's the

Outro

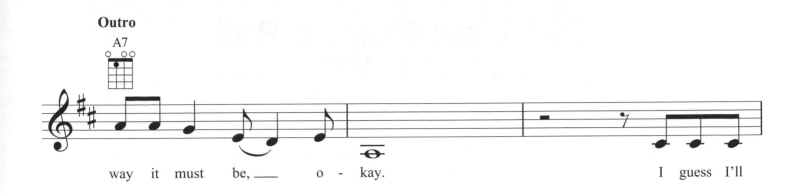

way it must be, ___ o - kay. I guess I'll

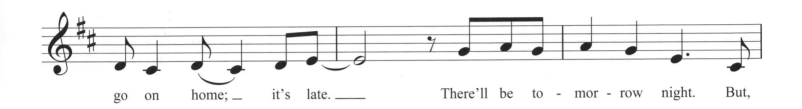

go on home; ___ it's late. ___ There'll be to - mor - row night. But,

wait! What do I see? _____

Is she walk - ing back to me? _____

___ Yeah, ___ she's walk - ing back to me! _____

___ Oh, _____ Pret - ty wom - an.

Old Time Rock & Roll

featured in RISKY BUSINESS

Words and Music by George Jackson and Thomas E. Jones III

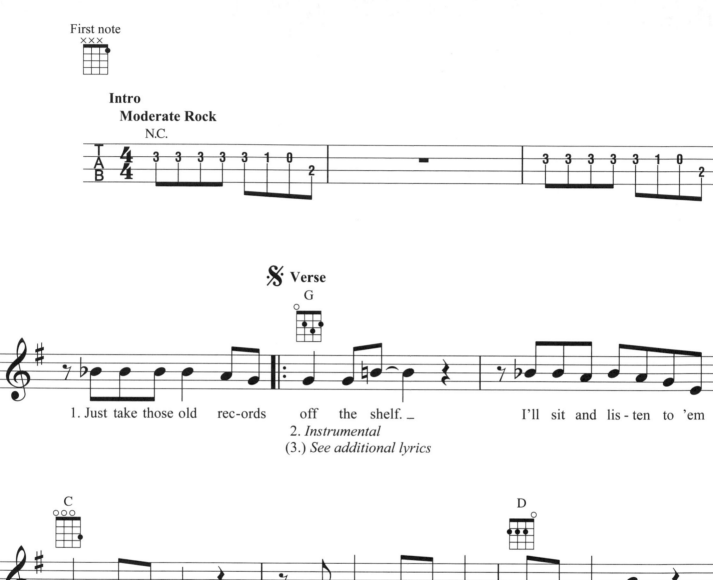

1. Just take those old rec-ords off the shelf. ___ I'll sit and lis-ten to 'em

2. *Instrumental*

(3.) *See additional lyrics*

by my - self. ___ To-day's mu - sic ain't got the same soul.

I like that old time ___ rock and roll. ___

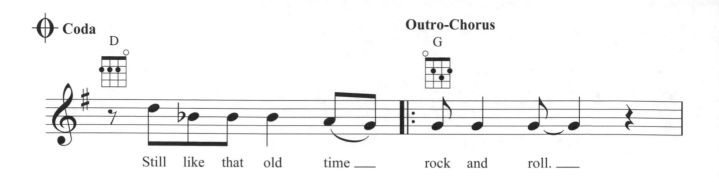

Coda

Outro-Chorus

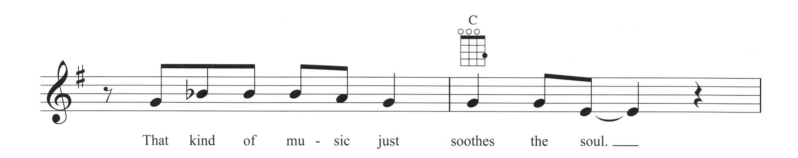

Still like that old time ___ rock and roll. ___

That kind of mu - sic just soothes the soul. ___

I rem - i - nisce a - bout the days of old ___

with that old ___ time rock and roll. ___ Still like that old time ___

Additional Lyrics

3. Won't go to hear 'em play a tango.
I'd rather hear some blues or funky old soul.
There's only one sure way to get me to go:
Start playin' old time rock and roll.
Call me a relic, call me what you will.
Say I'm old-fashioned, say I'm over the hill.
Today's music ain't got the same soul.
I like that old time rock and roll.

The Rainbow Connection

from THE MUPPET MOVIE
Words and Music by Paul Williams and Kenneth L. Ascher

First note

Verse
Flowing Waltz tempo

1. Why are there so man-y songs a-bout rain-bows and
2., 3. *See additional lyrics*

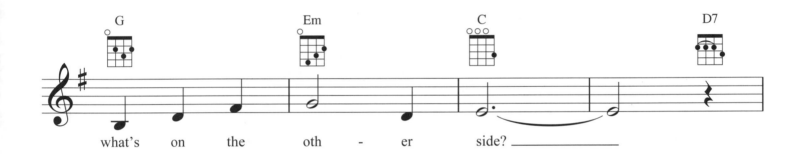

what's on the oth - er side? _____

Rain - bows are vi - sions, ___ but on - ly il - lu - sions, and

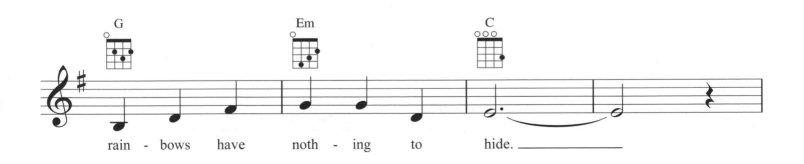

rain - bows have noth - ing to hide. _____

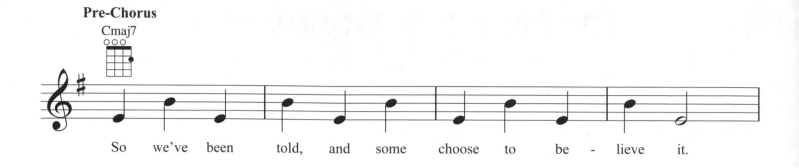

Pre-Chorus

So we've been told, and some choose to be - lieve it.

I know they're wrong; wait and see. _____

Chorus

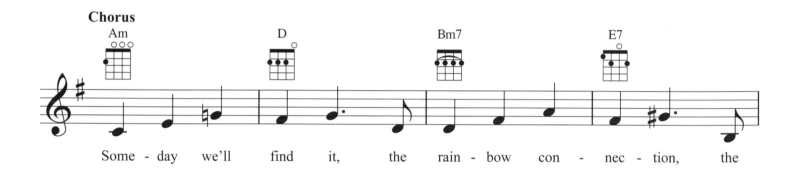

Some - day we'll find it, the rain - bow con - nec - tion, the

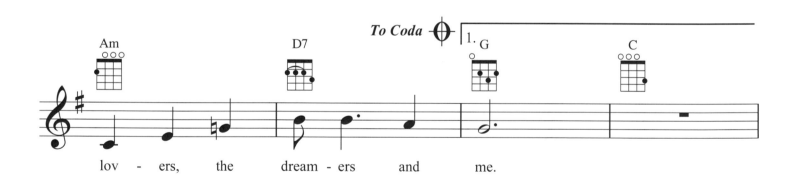

lov - ers, the dream - ers and me.

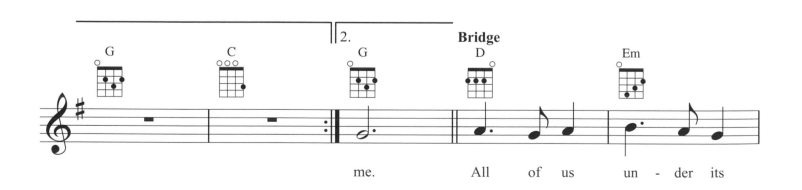

me. All of us un - der its

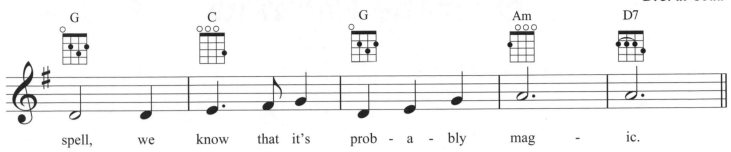

spell,   we   know   that   it's   prob - a - bly   mag   -   ic.

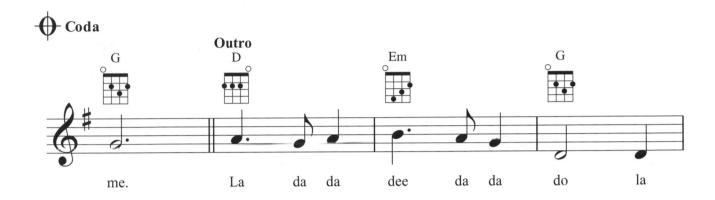

Coda

Outro

me.   La   da   da   dee   da   da   do   la

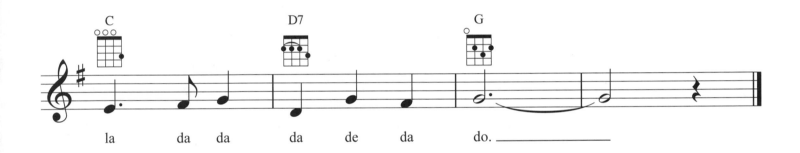

la   da   da   da   de   da   do. ____

Additional Lyrics

2. Who said that ev'ry wish would be heard and answered
   When wished on the morning star?
   Somebody thought of that and someone believed it;
   Look what it's done so far.
   What's so amazing that keeps us stargazing,
   And what do we think we might see?

3. Have you been half asleep and have you heard voices?
   I've heard them calling my name.
   Is this the sweet sound that calls the young sailors?
   The voice might be one and the same.
   I've heard it too many times to ignore it;
   It's something that I'm s'posed to be.

Over the Rainbow

from THE WIZARD OF OZ
Music by Harold Arlen
Lyric by E.Y. "Yip" Harburg

First note

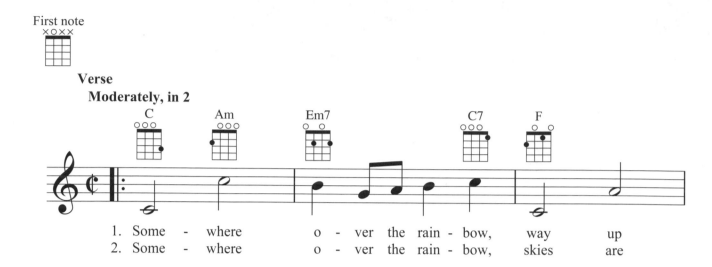

Verse
Moderately, in 2

1. Some - where o - ver the rain - bow, way up
2. Some - where o - ver the rain - bow, skies are

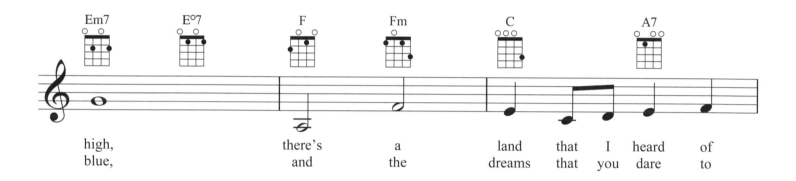

high, there's a land that I heard of
blue, and the dreams that you dare to

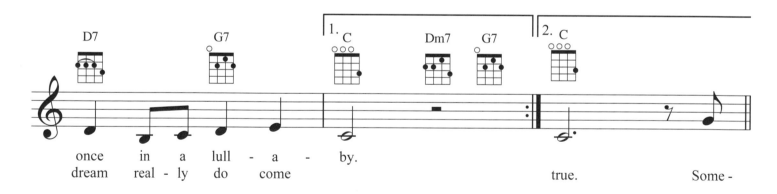

1. once in a lull - a - by.
   dream real - ly do come
2. true. Some -

Bridge

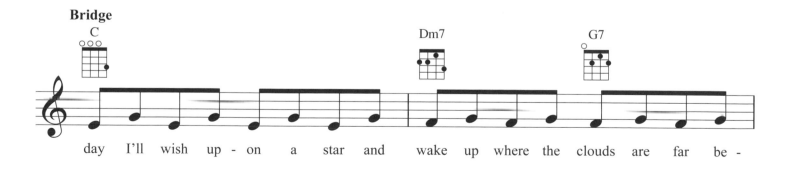

day I'll wish up - on a star and wake up where the clouds are far be -

hind me. _____ Where trou-bles melt like lem-on drops, a-way, a-bove the chim-ney tops; that's where you'll find me.

Verse

3. Some - where o - ver the rain - bow, blue - birds fly. Birds fly o - ver the rain - bow,

Outro

why, then, oh, why can't I? If hap-py lit-tle blue-birds fly be-yond the rain-bow, why, oh, why can't I? _____

Somewhere Out There

from AN AMERICAN TAIL

Music by Barry Mann and James Horner
Lyric by Cynthia Weil

far a-part we are, it helps to think we might be wish-in'

on the same bright star. And when the night wind starts to sing that

lone-some ___ lull-a-by, it helps to think we're sleep-ing un-der-

Outro-Verse

neath the same big sky. Some-where out there, if

love can see us through, then we'll be to-geth-er some-where

out there, out where dreams come true. _____

49

That's Amore
(That's Love)

from the Paramount Picture THE CADDY
Words by Jack Brooks
Music by Harry Warren

That's What Friends Are For

from NIGHT SHIFT
Music by Burt Bacharach
Words by Carole Bayer Sager

Time Warp

from THE ROCKY HORROR PICTURE SHOW
Words and Music by Richard O'Brien

1. It's as-tound-ing, ___ time ___ is fleet-ing, ___ mad-ness ___ takes its toll. But lis-ten close-ly ___ not for ver-y much long-er ___ I've got ___ to keep con-

trol. 2. I re-mem-ber ___ do-ing the Time ___

Warp, ___ drink - ing ___ those mo - ments when ___

___ the black - ness would hit me ___

and the void would be call - ing. ___ *All:* Let's do the

Time Warp a - gain. ___ Let's do the

Time Warp a - gain. ___ *Narrator:* It's just a jump to the left ___

Chorus

All: and then a step to the ri - i - i - i - i - ight.

Narrator: With your hands on your hips, ___   *All:* you bring your knees in

tight. ___   *Trio:* But it's the pel - vic thrust ___

that real - ly drives you in - sa - a - a - a - a - ane. ___

All: Let's   do   the   Time   Warp   a - gain. ___

To Coda ⊕

___   Let's   do   the   Time   Warp   a - gain. ___

Verse

___   *Magenta:* 3. It's   so   dream - y, ___   oh, fan - ta - sy

free __ me, ___ so you can't see me, ___ no, not at

all. In an-oth-er di-men - sion ___

with voy-eur-is-tic in-ten - tion, ___ well se-clud-ed ___

I'll see all. 4. With a bit of a mind flip ___

you're in-to the time _____ slip, ___ noth-ing ___

can ev-er be the same. ___ You're spaced out on sen-sa-tion ___

like you're un - der se - da - tion. ___   *All:* Let's   do   the

Time   Warp   a - gain. _____

Let's   do   the   Time   Warp   a - gain. _____

Bridge

Columbia: Well,   I   was   tap - ping down   the   street   just - a

hav - ing a   think, __   when   a   snake of   a   guy __ gave me an

e - vil wink. __   We - ell,   it   shook   me   up, ___   it   took me

by sur-prise, __ he had a pick-up truck __ and the dev-il's __ eyes. __ He

stared at me __ and I felt a change, __ time meant noth-ing, nev-er

would a - gain. __ *All:* Let's do the Time Warp a-

gain. _____ Let's do the

D.S. al Coda

Time Warp a - gain. _____ *Narrator:* It's just a jump to the left __

⊕ Coda

gain. _____

Twist and Shout

featured in the Motion Picture FERRIS BUELLER'S DAY OFF
Words and Music by Bert Russell and Phil Medley

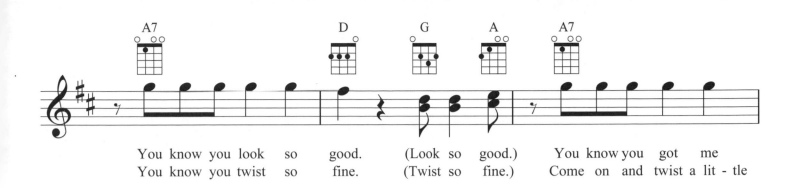

You know you look so good. (Look so good.) You know you got me
You know you twist so fine. (Twist so fine.) Come on and twist a lit - tle

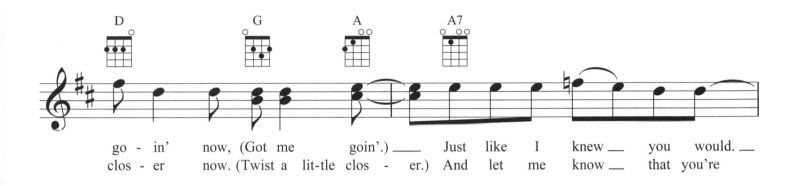

go - in' now, (Got me goin'.) ___ Just like I knew ___ you would. ___
clos - er now. (Twist a lit-tle clos - er.) And let me know ___ that you're

1. *To Coda*

2.

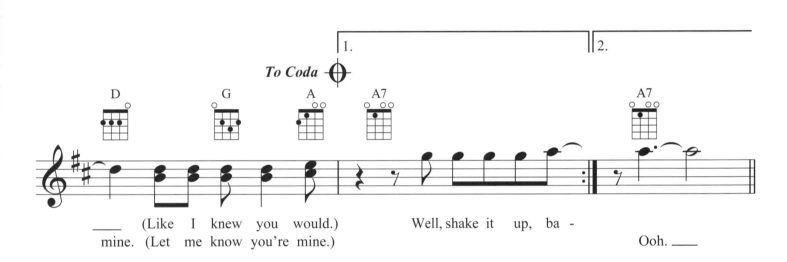

___ (Like I knew you would.) Well, shake it up, ba -
mine. (Let me know you're mine.) Ooh. ___

Interlude

Play 4 times

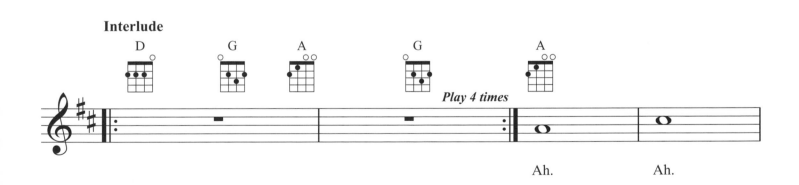

Ah. Ah.

D.S. al Coda

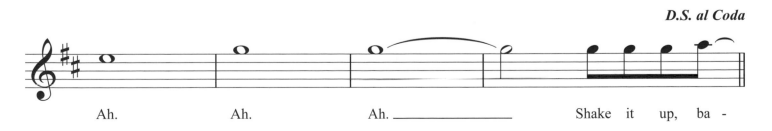

Ah. Ah. Ah. _____ Shake it up, ba -

Coda **Outro**

Well, shake it, shake it, shake it, ba - by, now.
(Shake it up, ba -

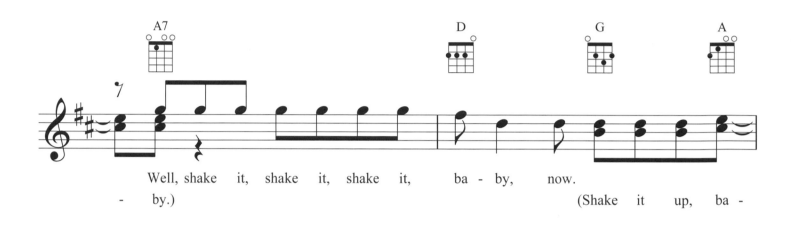

Well, shake it, shake it, shake it, ba - by, now.
- by.) (Shake it up, ba -

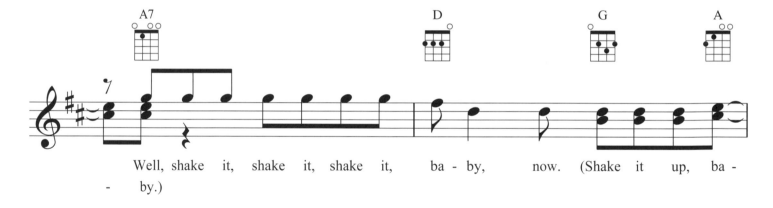

Well, shake it, shake it, shake it, ba - by, now. (Shake it up, ba -
- by.)

- by.) Ah. Ah.

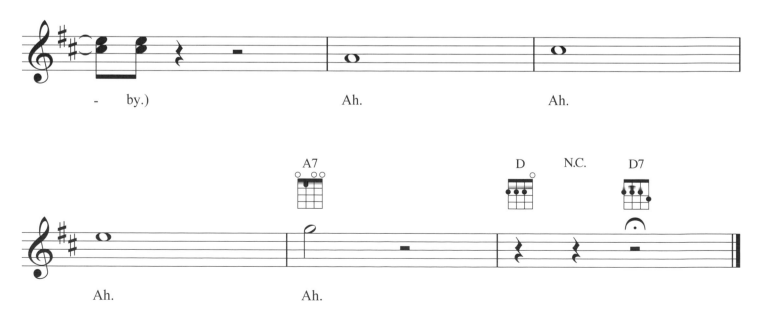

Ah. Ah.

Shout

featured in the Motion Picture ANIMAL HOUSE
Words and Music by O'Kelly Isley, Ronald Isley and Rudolph Isley

First note

Intro
Freely
N.C.

Well, _____

𝄋 Chorus 1
Moderately fast

you know you make me wan-na (Shout!) kick my heels up and (Shout!) throw my hands up and
(D.S.) (Shout!) (Shout!)

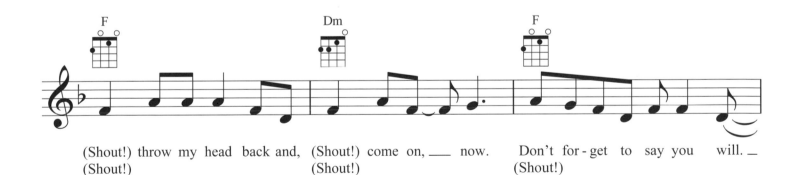

(Shout!) throw my head back and, (Shout!) come on, ___ now. Don't for-get to say you will. _
(Shout!) (Shout!) (Shout!)

_____ Don't for-get to say yeah, yeah, _ yeah, yeah, _ yeah.
(Shout!) (Shout!) (Shout!)

_____ (Shoo - be - doo.) yeah, _____ yeah. ___ I was a fool __ ____ for you from the bot - tom of my soul, ___ yeah. Now _____ that you've grown ____ up you're old, e - nough to know, _____ yeah, _____ yeah. _____ You wan - na leave ____ me. (Shoo - be doo - wop.) You wan - na let me go. ____ (Shoo - be doo - wop, doo - wop.) I want you to

Verse
Half-time feel

know,   I said I want you to know __ right now,   yeah,

you been good __ to me, ba - by, _____ bet - ter than I've been to my -

self,   yeah,   hey.   And if you ev - er   leave __ me, __ I don't

want   no - bod - y else,   hey,   hey.   I said I want you to know, __

_____ hey,   I said I want you to know __ right now, yeah,   yeah.

$\bigoplus$ **Coda**

D.S. al Coda

You know you make me wan - na

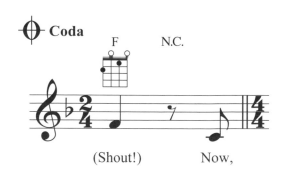

(Shout!)   Now,

One strum per chord, next 11 bars.

Outro

Repeat and fade

What the World Needs Now Is Love

featured in MY BEST FRIEND'S WEDDING

Lyric by Hal David
Music by Burt Bacharach

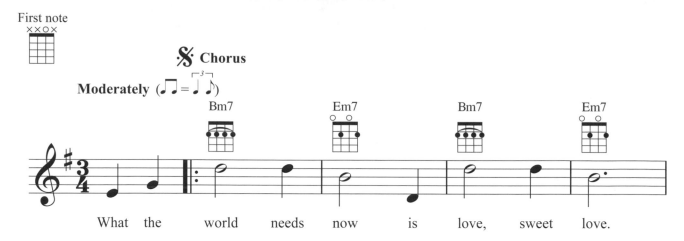

It's the on-ly thing _____ that there's just _____ too lit-tle of. What the

world needs now is love, sweet love. No, not just for some, _____

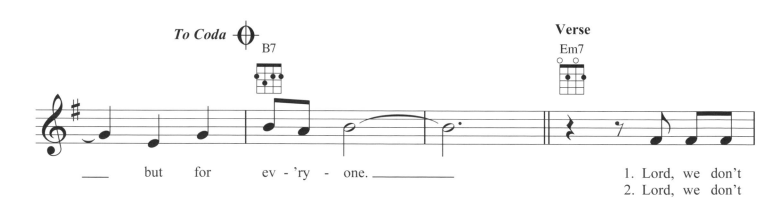

_____ but for ev-'ry-one. _____

1. Lord, we don't
2. Lord, we don't

The Windmills of Your Mind

Theme from THE THOMAS CROWN AFFAIR
Words by Alan and Marilyn Bergman
Music by Michel Legrand

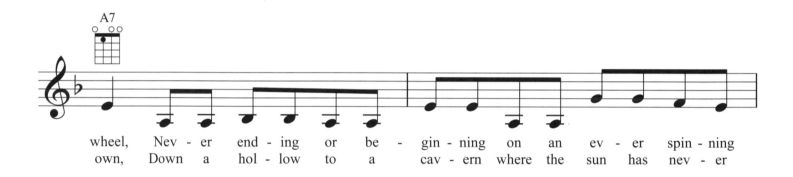

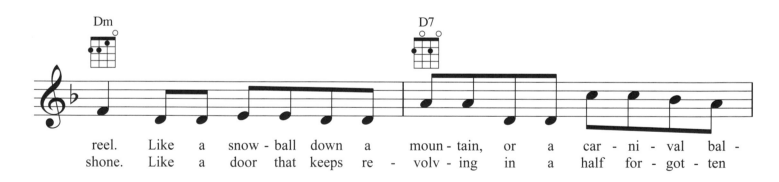

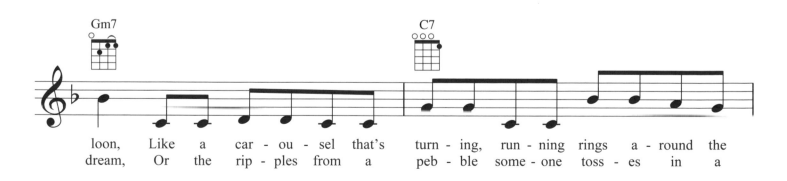

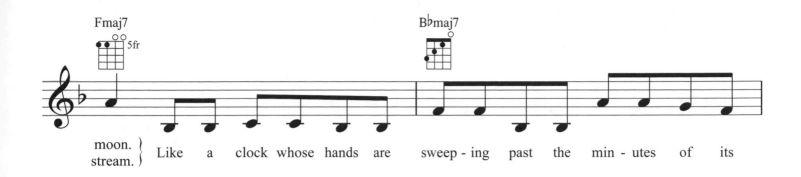

Fmaj7　　　　　　　　　　　　　　　Bbmaj7

moon.
stream.　Like　a　clock　whose　hands　are　sweep - ing　past　the　min - utes　of　its

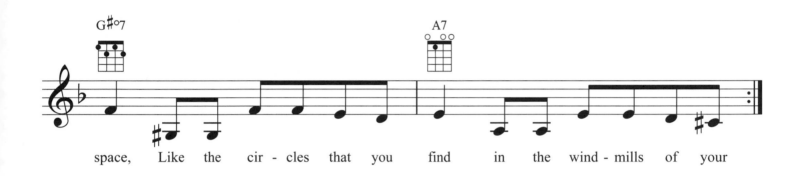

Em7b5　　　　　　　　　　　　　　　A7

face,　And　the　world　is　like　an　ap - ple　whirl - ing　si - lent - ly　in

G#°7　　　　　　　　　　　　　　　A7

space,　Like　the　cir - cles　that　you　find　in　the　wind - mills　of　your

Verse

Dm

mind!　3. Keys　that　jin - gle　in　your　pock - et,　words　that　jan - gle　in　your

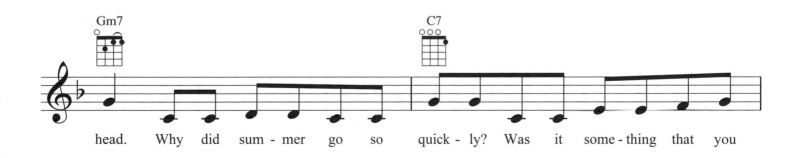

Gm7　　　　　　　　　　　　　　　C7

head.　Why　did　sum - mer　go　so　quick - ly?　Was　it　some - thing　that　you

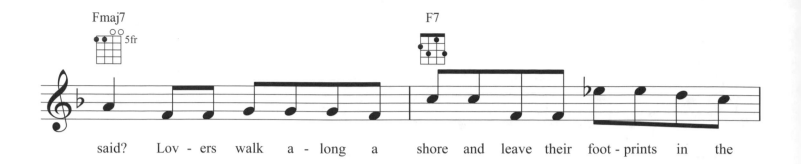

said? Lov - ers walk a - long a shore and leave their foot - prints in the

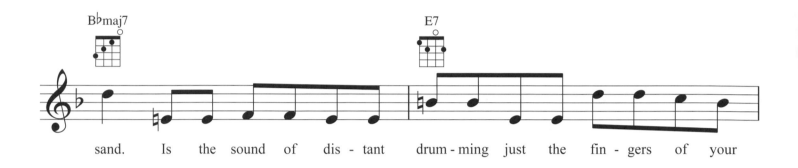

sand. Is the sound of dis - tant drum - ming just the fin - gers of your

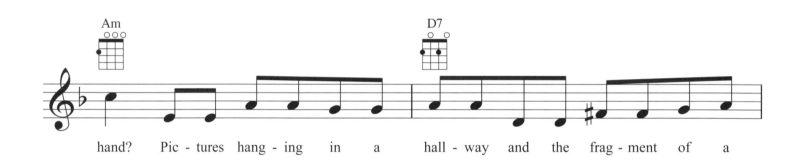

hand? Pic - tures hang - ing in a hall - way and the frag - ment of a

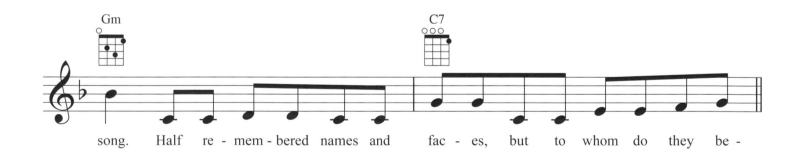

song. Half re - mem - bered names and fac - es, but to whom do they be -

Outro

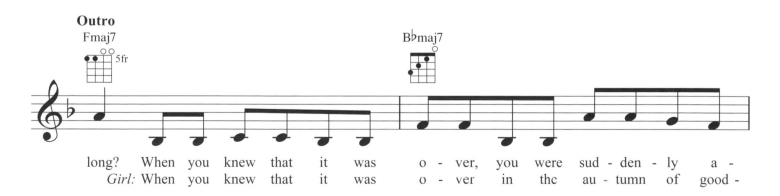

long? When you knew that it was o - ver, you were sud - den - ly a -
Girl: When you knew that it was o - ver in the au - tumn of good -

ware   That the au - tumn leaves were   turn - ing to the col - or of her
byes,   For a mo - ment you could   not re - call the col - or of his

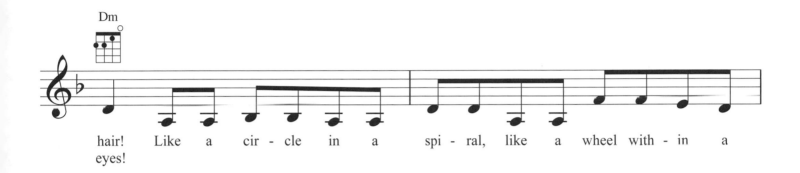

hair! Like a cir - cle in a   spi - ral, like a wheel with - in a
eyes!

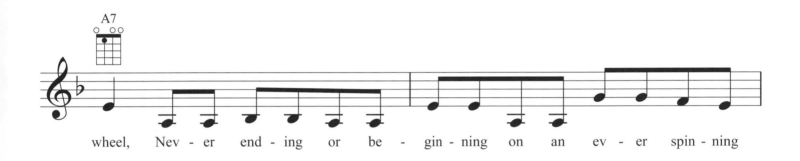

wheel, Nev - er end - ing or be - gin - ning on an ev - er spin - ning

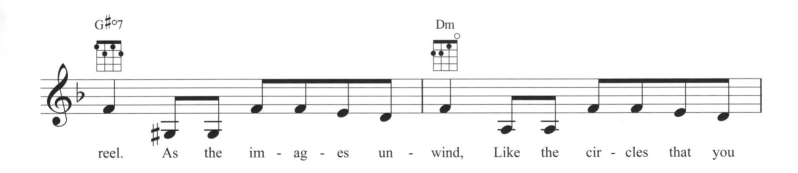

reel.   As the im - ag - es un - wind, Like the cir - cles that you

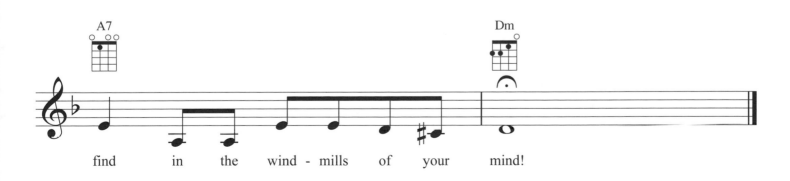

find   in the wind - mills of your mind!

You Light Up My Life

from YOU LIGHT UP MY LIFE
Words and Music by Joseph Brooks

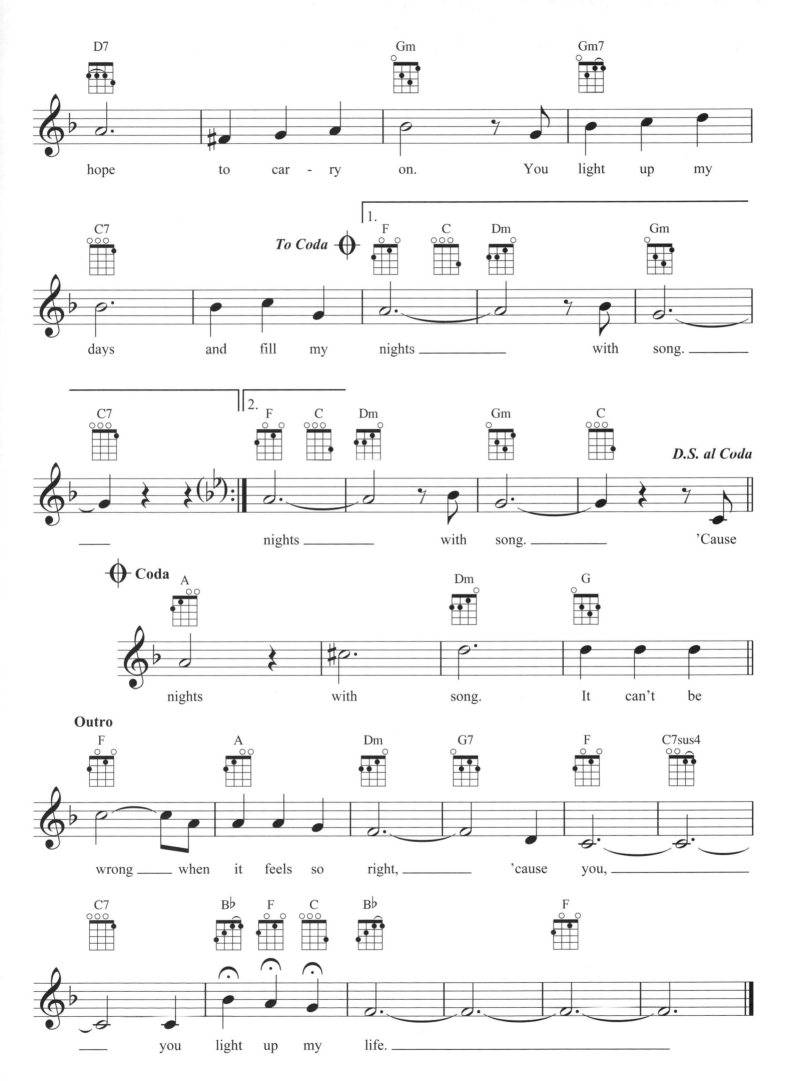

The Wind Beneath My Wings

from the Original Motion Picture BEACHES
Words and Music by Larry Henley and Jeff Silbar

1. It must have been cold ___ there in my shad - ow,
2., 3. *See additional lyrics*

to nev - er have sun - light on your

face.

You were con - tent ___

___ to let me shine; that's your way. ___

You al - ways walked ___ a step be - hind.

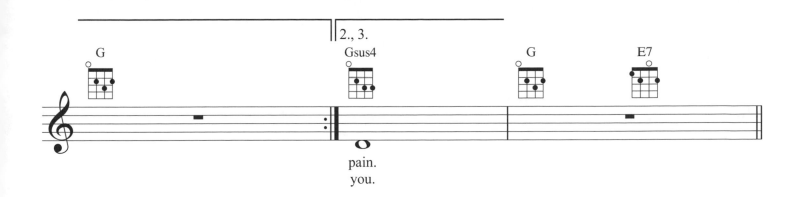

pain.
you.

𝄋 Chorus

Did you ev - er know _____ that you're my he - ro
Did you ev - er know _____ that you're my he - ro?

and ev - 'ry - thing I _____ would like to
You're ev - 'ry - thing I _____ wish I could

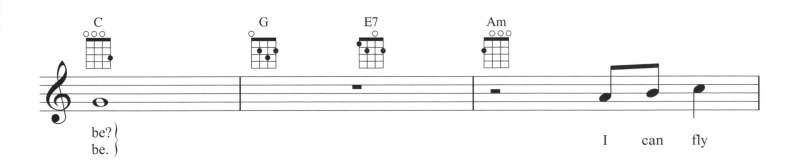

be?
be.

I can fly

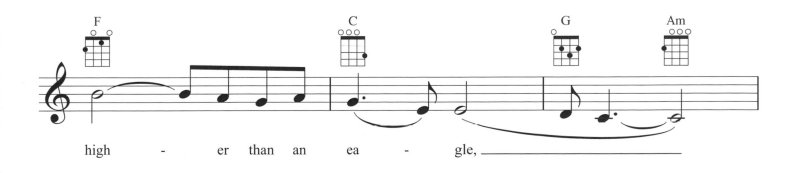

high - er than an ea - gle, _____

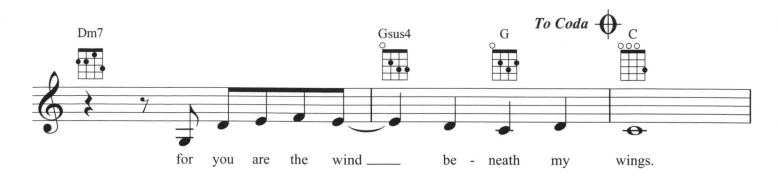

for you are the wind ____ be - neath my wings.

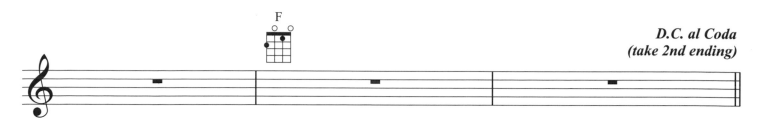

D.C. al Coda
(take 2nd ending)

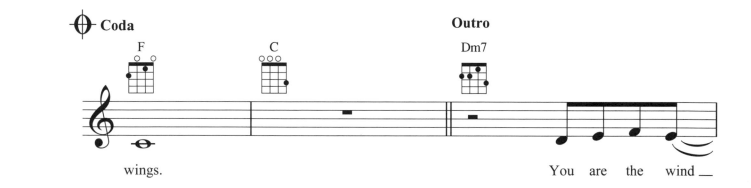

Coda   **Outro**

wings.   You are the wind ___

_____ be - neath my wings. _____

Additional Lyrics

2. So I was the one with all the glory,
   While you were the one with all the strength.
   A beautiful face without a name for so long,
   A beautiful smile to hide the pain.

3. It might have appeared to go unnoticed,
   But I've got it all here in my heart.
   I want you to know I know the truth, of course I know it.
   I would be nothing without you.